Charles Bridge

by
Zdeněk Dragoun
Jiřina Šebková

OSWALD

Text © Zdeněk Dragoun (pgs. 11—72)
   © Z. Dragoun's texts sumarized Jiřina Šebková (pgs. 3—10)
Photographs © Zdeno Feyfar (pgs. 23, 55, 69)
       © František Malý
       © Vojtěch Obereigner (cover, pgs. 21, 63, 68)
Translation © Ludmila Caravanasová
       © Hana Hubáčková
Design © Bohumil Karas
Editor Helena Osvaldová
Published by OSWALD, 1st Edition 1991
Printed in Czechoslovakia by GRAFIATISK Děčín
ISBN 80-900636-4-0

Charles bridge is one of Prague's best known and most significant historical monuments. Together with Prague Castle it is one of the most popular sights in the capital, and since they are commonly depicted together, Charles Bridge has become one of the symbols of the Prague panorama. Prague Castle and Charles Bridge are closely linked not only through the Emperor Charles IV and his architect Peter Parler, but above all in their parallel historical development.

As early as at the end of the 9th century a fort of the ruling Premyslids was founded on the left bank of the Vltava, at the place of the present Prague Castle. Below the castle a settlement soon developed, which ensured a general economic base for the princes' residence and for the traders' companies. During the 10th century this settlement also expanded to the right bank. The original crossings of the Vltava, where Prague is now located, were made across fords. The development of the settlements made closer and more freqent contacts between the banks of the Vltava necessary, so it was decided to build the first wooden Prague bridge.

The first written report refering to the existence of a bridge in Prague comes from the first half of the 10th century. In the so-called Kristian Legend a badly damaged bridge across the river Vltava is mentioned on the occasion of the transfer of St Wenceslas' body from Stará Boleslav to Prague Castle. Another written report about the bridge comes from Kosmas, the Dean of St Vitus' Church, in his Czech Chronicle. In this report he depicts a big flood in September 1118 which surged to a level of 15 feet (10 ells) above the bridge. We have no further information about the fate of the wooden bridge. We only know that in the second half of the 12th century it was replaced with a stone one.

Judith Bridge

Building activity in Romanesque Prague reached its peak during the reign of the Czech Prince, later the King, Vladislav I (1140—1172). By the end of his reign Prague was one of the most significant and impressive settlements in Central Europe. This could be seen in Prague Castle, built entirely of stone with fortifications secured by watch towers. Within the Castle there were also a number of churches including the spacious St Vitus' Basilica, St George's Convent and St Vitus' Chapter, along with the palaces of the prince and the bishop. Only a little less imposing was the princes' residence of Vyšehrad. In the settlement round the Castle and in different communities between the princes' forts, we can count dozens of Romanesque churches including large monasterial ones. A number of all-stone Romanesque houses were built within the, at that time unfortified, settlement around the Castle. Some of these formed the heart of large aristocratic or religious palaces.

At Fridrich Barbarossa's side, Vladislav spent much time outside Bohemia but his loyalty to the Emperor was fruitfull. In 1158 he was granted a royal title and Prince Vladislav II became King Vladislav I. He decided to celebrate his coronation by building a stone bridge. He modelled it after the oldest stone bridge in Europe, the bridge located in Regensburg. It is supposed that the same builders as in Regensburg took part in the construction of Prague Bridge as well. Even after his coronation the duties of the imperial court apparently kept Vladislav from residing in Bohemia frequently. But fortunately there was his second wife Judith Thuringia who supervised the construction of the bridge and after whom the bridge was later named. According to the Prague Canon Vincentius' Chronicle, the bridge was built within three years.

The Romanesque bridge was situated in close proximity to Charles Bridge, its Lesser Quarter base corresponded exactly to that of Charles Bridge. Altogether this 514m long construction spanned the Vltava in several slightly broken sections of 21—22 arches.

Most of the bridge was 7,5 m wide, but there were parts with a width of more than 10m. On both sides of the bridge there was a stone parapet, roughly 1m high and 35cm wide.

The basic building material was red and greenish sandstone, formed into big ashlar blocks, some of which were more than 1m long. Within the mass of the masonry other different kinds of stone were also used.

Both ends of the bridge were protected by towers and gates. The Lesser Quarter side near the bridge was in addition to this protected by significant religious buildings — south of the bridge by the monasterial complex of the Knights of St John and on the northern side by the Bishop's Palace. At the time of the completion of the bridge, in about 1172, probably only the Lesser Quarter bank was thoroughly protected, while the settlement on the Old Town bank was not so important. Simultaneously, a tower was built above the first right-bank pier, surviving up to the present time in the risalit of the Knights of the Cross' hospital. Only a torso of the Romanesque bridge has been preserved for the present and future generations.

The only monumental part of Judith Bridge apparent at first sight is the smaller Lesser Quarter Bridge Tower. It used to be one of two Romanesque bridge towers with a gate between them leading to the bridge. On the first floor, we can see the well known Romanesque bridge relief, which represents the peak Romanesque sculpture in Bohemia and ranks among prominent works of Central

Europe sculpture from that time. Two statues are presented on the relief in the shallow recess situated on the eastern part of the tower. They may represent King Vladislav I and the builder of the bridge kneeling in front of him, or the reconciliation between King Wenceslas I and his rebellious son, later the Iron and Golden King, Přemysl Otakar II, or the celebration of the founding of the Lesser Quarter in 1257 (a locator of the city kneels in front of Přemysl Otakar II). The most recent expert evaluation explained the scene as the bestowing of the royal title on the then Czech Prince Vladislav II by Friedrich Barbarossa.

A part of the original decoration was so-called Bradáč. It is a human head which is, according to a popular legend, regarded as a self-portrait of the builder of the bridge. It was placed in such a position that is served as a danger sign marking the water level during floods. After the reconstruction in 1847 the sculpture was set into the newly built embankment wall at the same height above the Vltava as it had previously been.

Further fragments of Judith Bridge have survived in the residential area on the Lesser Quarter bank, especially under the paving of local streets and in the facades of houses in the street At Lusatian Seminary.

In many reports from the 13th century we notice references to some events on the bridge, including incidents nearly of a bizarre character. One such incident is the death of the Knight Pertold, killed in 1250 by a stone which was dropped by two ravens from the highest part of what was probably the prison in the Lesser Quarter Bridge Tower.

The battles of those days did not seem to damage the bridge severely. The Vltava's force during big floods represented a greater danger. In February 1342 high water levels sealed the bridge's fate. The bridge broke in several places, and according to witnesses hardly one third of it remained. "It seemed that the crown of the kingdom fell when the glorious bridge collapsed" wrote František Pražský, the contemporary chronicler.

Charles Bridge in the Gothic Era

Even at the time of his coronation as the Roman Emperor in 1349, Charles IV had already decided that Prague would be the capital of the Holy Roman Empire. This decision changed considerably both the role and appearance of medieval Prague. In the course of a short period at the beginning of his reign he not only supported further works on St Vitus's Cathedral, but also started a vast reconstruction of Prague Castle, founded Prague University and in the great urban plan enlarged Prague by founding the New Town. Due to Charles's activities, Prague became one of the most important European cities with the number of inhabitants reaching 40 000 people. The Prague royal and imperial court became the greatest cultural centre in the area east of the Alps. The town was visited by many outstanding contemporary celebrities, among others, Petrarca lived in Prague for some time. With the support of the royal court, Peter Parler's workshop developed its sculptural and building activity.

Charles's influence on life in the country was remarkably wide spread. He was highly educated, he spoke several languages, and wrote his own books. He also possessed tremendous collection of ecclesiastic relics. The area belonging to the Czech Kingdom was enlarged due to his intelligent diplomacy and profitable marriages. Charles Bridge ranks among the most important monuments preserved from that time. Its foundation stone was layed by the Emperor himself on July 9, 1357 on the Old Town bank and consequently a more generous construction began to rise, just to the south of the ruined Judith Bridge. But frequent floods slowed down the pace of the work and floods in 1367 damaged one of the bridge's piers.

We have no exact information regarding the precise date of completion of Charles Bridge. Charles IV had probably died before the bridge was completed. The toll was introduced as late as 1383 by Charles's successor King Wenceslas IV (1378—1419), which was five years after Charles's death. The bridge spans the Vltava's river-bed by 16 semi-circular vaulted arches. The total length of the bridge is 516m. The width of the bridge is nearly 10m and its route follows a slightly broken S-shaped line. Large sandstone blocks held in place with mortar and iron hooks were used to construct the bridge. The builder of the bridge and the Old Town Bridge Tower was Peter Parler, a Swabian from Gmünde, who came to Prague to continue the building of St Vitus's Cathedral, which had been started earlier by Matthias of Arras. Parler's workshop took part in several other building projects both in and outside of Prague. His brush-work is easily distinguishable especially on the monumental Old Town Bridge Tower.

The elegant prismatoid tower, reaching 40m above the roadway of the bridge ends in a gallery and battlement with 4 corner turrets. A chisel-shaped roof culminates in 2 golden globes with discs of the sun.

Artistically, the most valuable part of the Old Town Bridge Tower is its east front. A broken arch is lined with a profiled archivolt resting on figurative consoles. Just under the main ledge there are 10 coats-of-arms belonging to the lands of the Czech Kingdom. Starting on the left there are the arms of the dominions of Nisa, Vratislav and Svídnice and Moravian Margraviate. At the most important place from the heraldic point of view is a spread-eagle, an emblem of the Holy Roman Empire. On the right the Czech lion occupies the place of honour. The lion is followed by the arms of Zhořelec, Budyšín and Dolní Lužice. Their order corresponds to the position of dominions within the Czech Kingdom in 1373—1377.

The most conspicious decoration is on the first floor of the tower. It is concentrated in a triangular panel with St Vitus's figure standing on a model stone bridge. On both sides of the panel there are 2 figures on thrones. The left one, representing Charles IV, has a slightly inclined head creating an impression of old age and fatigue. On the right is young King Wenceslas IV. All the figures (including St Vitus) are holding symbols of sovereign power. Outside the field of the triangle there are reliefs of a kingfisher on a wreath. This decoration element is typical of works of art connected directly with Wenceslas IV.

The top part of the sculptural decoration of the tower is represented by 2 statues of saints — on the left is St Adalbert, on the right, St Sigismond. They date back to the late 1380s when the construction of the tower itself was finished.

Prague vistas from 1572 and 1606 depict scenes of the west front of the tower. From this information we can roughly reconstruct the main elements of its decoration which have not been preserved. The central figure used to be a standing Madonna and child, with two other figures lying at her feet, Charles IV with one of his wives. On the second floor there was most likely a pair of saints, St Wenceslas and St Ludmila.

Regarding the furnishing of the interior it is important to note a naturalistic statue of a so-called "towerman" on the top of the staircase. The wooden truss of the high roof is mainly in the Gothic style. Inside the archway we can recognize details reminding us of the original fortification role of the tower. There is, for example, a groove on the east side in the corner buttresses which was used to control a portcullis providing protection for the side of the tower facing the Old Town. Bulky iron rings at the west end of the archway were used to fasten a gate leading to the Lesser Quarter. Another element of defence is a coping stone. This beautifully carved stone is considered a magnificent crown to the vault. In addition to its grace and beauty, it had rather prosaic function. It was used as a so-called "pouring hole", by means of which defenders of the tower could pour boiling water or otherwise unpleasant liquids on the enemy.

Because the tower of the Romanesque bridge on the bank had been preserved, the builders could use it, and for that reason the point of entry to the Lesser Quarter remained the same.

Charles Bridge, at that time called Stone or Prague Bridge, became the scene of many events of importance in Prague history. The martyr's death of John of Nepomuk, a confessor to Queen Sophia, is one of the more tragic episodes. John of Nepomuk refused to give away a secret of the confession to the King and on March 20, 1393 was thrown from the bridge.

There were other events as well which were enjoyed especially by observers. One example is a strange punishment inflicted on dishonest traders. They are said to have been dipped in the Vltava in wicker baskets. Another occurance of this kind was a big tournament organized in 1436 on the bridge by Sigismond of Luxemburg, otherwise one of the least popular Kings in Czech history.

Although the new bridge was 4 — 5 m higher than the former one, it could not stand floods and breached in 1432. Its reconstruction took several decades mainly because of the stormy times marked by the Hussite wars. Beginning in 1464 simultaneous construction of the present higher Lesser Quarter Bridge Tower occured and the new tower replaced the northern Romanesque one. It was built under the strong influence of Parler's Old Town Bridge Tower and was most likely finished at the beginning of the 16th century. Its decoration is also concentrated on the east and west sides, repeating the three-scheme of sculptural decoration of the Old Town Bridge Tower.

On the battlement above the broken arches of the doorway are copies of original coats-of-arms belonging to the lands of the Czech Kingdom. The passage through the doorway is not vaulted, this enabled defenders to strike attackers from galleries on the first floor. At the end of the doorway close to the bridge are iron rings, on the other side is a groove for a portcullis.

Inside on the first floor are originals of the arms we have seen on the battlement. On the second floor we can find some architectural details replaced during Mocker's reconstruction in 1879—1893.

In the Gothic era the first statues, which have not been preserved, were erected. We have a written inscription reporting that as early as at the beginning of the 15th century there was a statue of the Crucified Christ. According to engravings from the 16th and 17th centuries, a later copy used to stand on the 4th pier from the Old Town bank. In the 15th century there was probably an equestrian statue of King George of Poděbrady. On the 16th pier from the Lesser Quarter bank is a statue of so-called "Bruncvík" created back in the early 16th century. "Bruncvík" is a knight in armour with a sword and shield resembling the figures of Rolands in German towns, which were to express the trade and customs rights of the towns.

Charles Bridge in the Baroque Era

The Renaissance style had little influence on the decoration of the bridge. The only exception was a reconstruction of the lower Lesser Quarter Bridge Tower in 1591 when it gained the present roof gables and sgrafitti.

It was the following Baroque century which influenced the bridge considerably. In 1611, at the Old Town Bridge Tower, troops of Passau mercenaries were stopped. These troops played a bloody role in the conflict between the Habsburg ruler Rudolph II (1576 — 1611) and his brother Matthias (1611 — 1619).

A few years later, in 1621, heads of executed Czech noblemen were displayed in an iron cage on the Old Town Bridge Tower. After the tower had been conquered by Swedish army their heads were taken away and buried by Czech protestants.

At the end of the Thirty Years' War, in 1648, the Swedish army led by general Königsmark, conquered the Lesser Quarter. Inspite of intensive bombardment they did not manage to conquer the Old Town Bridge Tower and enter the Old Town. At the time of an intense battle between the Swedes and catholic students a messenger turned up with a message about the Westphalian peace treaty. A month later in a wooden house in the middle of the bridge, Prague signed a truce as well.

Swedish artillery fire in 1648 did not cause much damage of the bridge itself, but it completely destroyed Parler's decoration on the west front of the Old Town Bridge Tower and seriously damaged a wooden Calvary and the statue of Bruncvík. The reconstruction of the tower in 1651—1654 was entrusted to an Italian architect Carlo Lurago. It was he who fitted a marble tablet with the Old Town arms and Latin inscription on the west front of the tower. This tablet depicts the expulsion of the Swedes. Though the wooden Calvary was restored it was soon replaced with a bronze Christ and later 3 flanking wooden statues were replaced with lead ones.

A statue of St John of Nepomuk, cast after a model by J. Brokoff was erected on the bridge on the occasion of the 300th anniversary of the Saint's death. The inscription below the statue fallaciously claims that the Saint died in 1383. In 1695 the first stone statue was fitted on the bridge above the same pier as the Calvary. The sculpture created by J. Brokoff was called the Pietà and it consisted of the Virgin Mary with Christ and a pair of angels. Today the sculpture is housed in the Pod Petřínem hospital, which was once the Convent of Sisters of Mercy of St Charles Bertolomew.

In about 1700 an Italian sculptor Ottavio Mosto created for the bridge a sculptured piece of St Wenceslas with two angels. In 1784 the piece was damaged by a flood.

Around 1700 there were 4 sculptures on the bridge. In the course of only nine years, in 1706—1714, a further 25 statues or sculptural groups were raised on the bridge. A great number of Baroque sculptors of different artistic conceptions took part in the bridge's decoration. Sites for separate sculptures were allocated by a bridge authority of the Old Town Hall and financial expences were covered by rich noblemen and officials.

Except for two bronze sculptures and one marble, all the others are carved from Czech sandstone.

The more humble and less dynamic school of Baroque sculpture is represented by Jan Bedřich Kohl (1681—1736). Apart from his sculptures on the bridge—St Augustine and St Nicholas of Tolentino — another well known work of his is a sculpture of St Felix on the porch outside the Prague Loretto. Another sculptor who took part in the decoration of the bridge was František Preiss with his sculptural group of St Francis of Assissi. After 1848 his sculptures were moved to the courtyard of a Capuchin church consecrated to St Joseph in the present Square of the Republic in the Prague New Town.

Jan Bedřich Mayer's contribution to the decoration of the bridge are statues of St Anthony of Padua, St Jude Taddeus as well as a sculptured piece of SS. Cosmas and Damian with the figure of Christ.

Bernard Mandl, a Salzburg sculptor of Czech origin, created for the bridge a statue of St Filip Benitius. Matěj Václav Jäckle (1655—1738) of Lusatian origin belonged to the older sculptural generation. Among other works he also created the sculptures for St Nicholas' Church in the Old Town Square. He contributed to the decoration of the bridge with 3 sculptures — the Madonna with SS. Dominic and Thomas Aquinas, the Madonna with St Bernard and a statue of St Anne.

The strongest influence on the bridge sculptural gallery was exercised by the Brokoffs—Jan (1650—1718) and his sons Jan Michael (1687—1721) and Ferdinand Maxmilian (1688—1731). Jan Brokoff created 5 sculptures for Charles Bridge but only one of them survived in its original position. It is one of the oldest bridge statues—a figure of John of Nepomuk. All the others were damaged.

All the Brokoffs participated in the creation of a sculptural group of St Barbara, St Elizabeth and St Margaret. The only statue which is supposed to have been solely created by J. M. Brokoff is that of St Adalbert.

The artistic activity of the family reached its climax in the works of F. M. Brokoff. In the course of 9 years he created 7 works, 6 of which are preserved. They are the large pieces depicting St Gaetano, St Francis Borgia, St Francis Xavier, St Ignatius of Loyola, SS. Vincent Ferrarius and Prokopius, St Vitus, and SS. John of Matha, Felix de Valois, and Ivan. The bridge lost only the group of St Ignatius of Loyola, which fell into the Vltava in a flood of 1890. A group with St Francis Xavier is considered the best of Brokoff's works.

The most important sculptor of the decoration on the bridge was Matthias Bernard Braun (1684—1738). A great number of his works were commissioned by his patron, Count Francis Anthony Špork. He reached his artistic climax in the sculptural decoration of the Kuks, where he created a gallery of statues expressing virtues and vices. He has only three representations on the bridge — St Ivo, St Ludmila and St Luitgarde. The latter being the most beautiful sculpture on Charles Bridge.

In the course of less than 10 years almost the whole tremendous sculptural decoration of the bridge was finished and as early as 1723 it was furnished with oil lighting.

Is was not until 1784 that floods did considerable damage to the bridge and the reconstruction of it claimed 150 000 gulden. During the reconstrunction, a staircase, connecting the bridge with Kampa Island, was built in 1785.

Modern history
of the Bridge

The first half of the 19th century was comparatively quiet. Moulded metal pavements were laid on the bridge in 1834—1835 and a Neogothic staircase leading to Kampa Island was built. In 1843—1848 the open space between the 1st Old Town arch of Charles Bridge was spanned, which resulted in an attractive open area. In this newly created space, known as Knights of the Cross Square an above size-life figure of Emperor Charles IV should have been set, having been cast after a model by Dresden sculptor E. J. Hähnel, on the occasion of the 500th anniversary of the foundation of Prague University. But armed clashes in June 1848 delayed its unveiling.

Prague Bridge became a battlefield again. But this time student guards did not resist the artillery fire of General Windischgrätze's army from the Lesser Quarter and failed to defend the Old Town Bridge Tower. The Bridge Tower together with 8 bridge statues were badly damaged.

First of all it was necessary to see to the Old Town Bridge Tower itself but soon itself but soon after that attention was paid to the sculptural decoration as well. In 1853—1861 the damaged statues were replaced with new ones in the Neogothic style as an attempt to conform to the architectural style of the bridge.

Josef Max (1804—1855) created a sculpture of SS. Norbert, Wenceslas and Sigismond and statues of St Joseph and St John the Baptist. His brother Emanuel Max chiseled sculptures of St Francis of Seraphicus, St Christopher and statues of the Virgin Mary and St John at the Calvary. A statue of St Wenceslas is a contribution by one of J. Max's followers, Joseph Kamil Böhm (1828—1862).

After the statue of Charles IV had been unveiled the bridge began to be called Charles Bridge more and more commonly. The name was officially confirmed in 1870.

During reconstruction in 1874—1880, a wooden Neogothic panelled ceiling was fitted on the second floor of the Old Town Bridge Tower. Frescoes in its archway were repainted and the Prague coat-of-arms was added to them.

The last disasterous flood struck Charles Bridge in 1890. The force pulled down two piers and breached three arches. Traffic on the bridge restarted as late as 1892. The crashed sculpture of St Francis Xaverius was replaced with its copy. Instead of the damaged sculptural group of Ignatius of Loyola a group of SS. Cyril and Methodius by Karel Dvořák (1893—1950) was erected.

Increasing traffic started to cause still greater difficulties. The bridge was used even by trams and cars. Since 1974, when the last reconstruction was finished, the bridge has been used only by pedestrians and represents the most impressive part of the Royal Way and the eternal symbol of Prague.

The sculptural decoration of Charles Bridge

The sculpture of the Madonna with St Bernard

The original by M. V. Jäckl of 1709 was replaced with a copy by V. Hlavatý, M. Vajchr, J. Vitvar, A. Viškovská, M. Tomšej and J. Wolf in the years 1976 to 1979. The sculpture was paid for by B. Litwerig, the Abbot of the Cistercian Monastery at Osek.

St Bernard of Clairvaux (1090—1153) was the founder of the Cistercian Order.

The Virgin Mary, with the Infant Jesus on her left arm and a sceptre in her right hand, stands in the middle of the group. St Bernard, wearing a vestment of the Cistercian Order, sits on the right, one of the cherubs holds his abbot's mitre. On the left plinth other cherubs carry the cross, below it on the plinth are the tools of the Crucifixion.

The sculpture of St Ivo

The original by M. B. Braun of 1711 was replaced by the sandstone copy by F. Hergesell in 1908. The work was paid for by the Law Faculty of Prague University.

St Ivo (†1303), the representative of religious justice, was known as the patron of the needy, particularly widows and orphans. He was also the patron of lawyers and of Prague University's Law Faculty.

The figure of the Saint, wearing the robes of a university professor and holding the Legal Code in his right hand, stands in the centre. From the right a group of clients look up to him and on the left behind him is the allegorical figure of Justice. The cartouche below the statue depicts St Ivo celebrating mass for the reconciliation between the mother and her son.

The sculpture of the Madonna with SS. Dominic and Thomas Aquinas

The original by M. V. Jäckl of 1708 was replaced by the copy by V. Bartůněk and S. Hanzl in the years 1960 to 1961. The erection of the sculpture was funded by the Dominican Abbey of St Giles of the Old Town of Prague.

St Dominic (1170—1221) was the founder of the Dominican Order and St Thomas Aquinas (1225—1274) its distinguished member and philosopher.

In the central part of the sculpture the Virgin Mary with the Infant Jesus stands amid clouds above the globe. On the left the figure of St Dominic holds out his hand to the Virgin Mary. St Thomas Aquinas, on the right, hands an open book to the Virgin Mary. The chronogram 1708 is repeated twice in the cartouches below St Dominic and St Thomas.

The sculpture of SS. Barbara, Margaret and Elizabeth

This work by Jan, Jan Michal and Ferdinand Maxmilián Brokoff dates from 1707, in 1852 it was repaired by J. Max. The erection of the sculpture was made possible by the imperial councillor Jan Václav Obytecký from Obytce.

St Barbara was a legendary Christian martyr, who lived in the 3rd century AD. She was held in a tower because of her faith and in the end beheaded by her own father. St Margaret suffered the same fate in 260 AD. According to legend, while in prison, by making the sign of the cross, she drove off the Devil, who took the form of a dragon. St Elizabeth (1207—1231), the daughter of the Hungarian King Andrew II, was recognized for caring for the poor and the sick.

St Barbara, with the crown a martyr, a chalice and a tower, stands in the middle. To the left of her is the figure of St Margaret, again with the crown a martyr, and with a cross and a dragon. On the right is St Elizabeth with the symbols of a ruler giving alms to a poor man. The coats-of-arms of the donor and his wife are below SS. Margaret and Elizabeth.

The sculpture of the Holy Cross — the Calvary

This is on the site of the original Gothic Calvary. The different ages of its separate parts reflect its complicated history. The bronze Christ was bought in Dresden in 1657, and was placed on a wooden cross in 1659. The Hebrew inscription around the cross dates from 1696, and in 1707 it was, together with the bronze Christ, placed on a new bronze cross. The inscripcions in Czech, Latin and German below the cross also date from 1707 and they say that the Hebrew inscription on the cross was added as a result of the fine paid by an unnamed Jew who blasphemed against the cross. On the marble pedestal of 1681, the wish of Karel Adam Lev from Říčany, to have an ever-burning light placed in front of the Calvary, is expressed.

The statues by E. Max of 1861 — on the left the Virgin Mary and on the right John the Evangelist, complement the sculpture.

The sculpture of the Pietà

The sculpture of the Pietà by J. Brokoff of 1695 was replaced by that of E. Max in 1859. A public collection funded its construction.

The figure of Christ leans on the Virgin Mary, on the right kneels St Mary Magdalene. John the Apostle stands above the three figures.

The statue of St Anne

The statue by M. V. Jäckl dates from 1707 and was paid for by Count Rudolf of Lisov. St Anne, the mother of the Virgin Mary, holds the Infant Jesus, who is giving a blessing, on her left arm and looks at the youthful-looking Virgin Mary. On the lower part of the plinth are the coats-of-arms of the donor and his wife.

The statue of St Joseph

This work by J. Max of 1854 was donated by the merchant J. Bergmann. Joseph holds a lily in his left hand and by his side stands the Infant Jesus, who is giving his blessing.

The sculpture of SS. Cyril and Methodius

The group by K. Dvořák was paid for by the Ministry of Education in 1938.

In the 9th century, in Moravia, SS. Cyril and Methodius, brothers from Thessaloniki, spread Christianity in the Slavonic language and they devised for the recording of religious texts their own alphabet.

The sculpture shows both Saints baptizing a group of three young heathens.

The sculpture of St Ignatius of Loyola by F. M. Brokoff of 1711, fragments of which are in the Lapidary (antique stone collections) of the National Museum, used to be here.

The sculpture of St Francis Xavier

The original by F. M. Brokoff of 1711 was replaced by Č. Vosmík's copy in 1913 and its fragments were deposited in the lapidary of the National Museum. The sculpture was paid for by the Theological and Philosophical Faculty of Prague University.

St Francis Xavier (1506—1552) worked as

a missionary in Eastern Asia from 1541 till his death. He converted thousands of inhabitants of India, Japan and China to Christianity. He became the patron saint of missionaries and seafarers.

The statute of St Francis, baptizing an Indian ruler, stands on the pedestal supported by the robust figures of a Chinese man, a Tartar, an Indian and a Moor. A young man with a conch, in which the water is prepared for baptism, and a man with a book wearing a coat, whose face bears a resemblance to F. M. Brokoff's, are looking at the scene.

The statue of St John the Baptist

The statue by J. Max of 1855 was financed by Prague burgher Jan Norbert Gemerich from Neuberg.

St John is depicted here as a preacher in the desert, wearing a sheep's pelt and a coat. The cross in his left hand and the conch at his side remind us of the baptism of Christ.

The sculpture of Christ's baptism by J. Brokoff of 1706 used to be here.

The statue of St Christopher

The statue by E. Max was financed by the burgomaster V. Wank in 1857.

According to legend St Christopher was a heathen giant, who converted to Christianity. As penance he had to carry pilgrims over the river at places where there were no bridges. It was at one such place that he once carried the Infant Jesus. He is the patron saint of pilgrims.

The larger than life figure of St Christopher, with a stick in his left hand and the Infant Jesus on his shoulder, steps on to land.

The unrealized memorial to Charles VI by M. Braun was to have been at this point. Later there was a military guard-house,

which collapsed into the Vltava.

Between the statue of St John the Baptist and the sculpture of St Norbert, on the right hand side of the bridge, there is a double cross, with stars at both ends of the horizontal arms and at the top, which shows the place where, according to legend, St John of Nepomuk was thrown into the Vltava.

The sculpture of SS. Norbert, Wenceslas and Sigismond

The statue of this group was made by J. Max in 1853 and paid for by J. Zeidler, the Abbot at Strahov Abbey.

St Norbert (1085—1134) was the Archbishop of Magdeburg and founder of the Premonstratensian Order. Since 1626, when his relics were taken to Strahov, he has been considered as one of Bohemia's patron saints. Alongside the Přemyslid Saint Wenceslas, the main patron saint of the Bohemian Kindom, St Sigismond (†523 AD) is also one of Bohemia's patron saints. Charles IV brought the relics of this Christian Burgundian king to Prague and laid them in St Vitus' Cathedral.

The statue of St Norbert stands in the centre among the armed Saints of the sovereign, St Wenceslas on the left and St Sigismond on the right. The precedent for St Wenceslas was Parler's sculpture in the St Wenceslas Chapel of St Vitus' Cathedral.

The statue of St Norbert by Max is the third on this site. Originally there was J. Brokoff's work of 1708, which was damaged in 1765 and replaced by the sculpture made by I. F. Platzer the elder. That was destroyed in 1848.

The sculpture of St Francis Borgia

F. M. Brokoff's work of 1710 was paid for

by František Collet, the imperial burgrave.

St Francis Borgia (1510—1572) was the Spanish duke, who, after the death of his wife, entered the Jesuit Order and became its third General.

The Saint is depicted here wearing the vestments of the Jesuit Order with a biretta on his head. The pair of angels on either side of him hold illustrations of the altar host and the Virgin Mary. On the plinth of the sculpture the course of St Francis' life is depicted allegorically, and on the pedestal of his statue is the coat-of-arms of the donor.

The statue of St John of Nepomuk

The bronze sculpture of St John of Nepomuk was cast by W. H. Heroldt in Nuremberg in 1683 copying J. Brokoff's wooden statue. That was made in 1682 after the small model produced by M. Rauchmüller, a Viennese sculptor. The reliefs on the plinth were cast following J. Mathey's design. The foundation of the statue was financed by Matyáš Wunšvic.

John of Pomuk (1345—1395), the Vicar General of the archdiocese of Prague, who according to legend received the confession of Queen Sophia, the wife of Wenceslas IV, was thrown into the Vltava for refusing to reveal the details of her confession. The figure of St John of Nepomuk, wearing a canon's robes and with a biretta on his head, with the palm branch of a martyr and a crucifix in his hands, set the precedent for further depictions of the Saint.

On the relief to the left is Queen Sophia at confession and King Wenceslas IV in front, on the right is John of Nepomuk being thrown into the Vltava. The Latin inscription mentions that the statue was erected on the occasion of the 300th anniversary of the martyr's death.

The sculpture of St Ludmila

This work by M. B. Braun of 1730 was placed on the bridge after the year 1784.

St Ludmila (†921 AD) was the wife of Bořivoj, the first baptized Přemyslid prince. Drahomíra, her heathen daughter-in-law, being afraid of Ludmila's influence upon young Wenceslas, arranged for her to be strangled.

St Ludmila si depicted as a princess with a prince's cap, holding a veil, a symbol of her martyr's death. Little Wenceslas, also wearing a prince's cap, is learning to read the Bible. A cherub sits on the right hand side of the plinth, the relief depicting the murder of St Wenceslas is in the middle of the scene.

In the same place there was previously a sculpture of St Wenceslas by O. Mosto. It was damaged by a flood in 1784. Its fragments are in the Lapidary of the National Museum today.

The statue of St Anthony of Padua

J. O. Mayer's statue of 1707 was paid for by K. M. Witthauer.

St Anthony of Padua (1195—1231) was a member of the Minorite Order and gained renown through his preaching.

The Saint is depicted wearing Minorite vestments and holding a lily in his hand; the Infant Jesus stands on a book which lies on a lectern. There is an incription with the date 1707 on the plinth, two vases showing scenes from the life of Anthony are on either side of the statue.

The sculpture of St Francis Seraphicus

The sculpture by E. Max originates from 1855 and was made to commemorate the survival of the Emperor Francis Joseph I after an assassination attempt in 1853, and was funded by Count František Kolowrat-Libštejnský.

St Francis of Assisi (1182—1226) was the founder of the Minorite, or Franciscan, Order (of the lesser brothers of St Francis), who followed his ideal of a life of poverty.

The Saint, wearing Minorite vestments, stands between two angels holding the cross and the Gospels.

The statue of St Jude of Thaddeus

This work by J. O. Mayer of 1708 was paid for by František Sezima from Mitrovice.

St Jude of Thaddeus, one of the Apostles, died as a martyr while spreading the Christian faith.

The robust figure of the Saint is depicted with a book in his right hand and a sizeable club in his left hand, the tool of his martyrdom. The date 1708 is on the plinth.

The sculpture of SS. Vincent Ferrarius and Procopius

The sculpture is the work of F. M. Brokoff and was funded by Count Romedius František Thun in 1712.

St Vincent (1357—1419) was a member of the Dominican Order and is remembered for converting unbelievers to Christianity. St Procopius (†1053), one of Bohemia's patron saints, was the first Abbot of Sázava Monastery. According to legend, near to the monastery he ploughed together with the devil harnessed to the plough, the so-called "Devil's furrow".

St Vincent stands on top of the coffin and resuscitates the corpse in the left part of the sculpture. A repentant sinner bows down in front of St Vincent. A relief of the Last Judgement is on the plinth between the figures of the Saracen and the Jew, who were the particular recipients of his converting zeal.

The right hand part of the sculpture is dedicated to St Procopius, depicted here with an abbot's mitre and holding a crosier above the defeated Satan. The third figure on the plinth is Satan, and between him and the figure of the Jew is the legendary scene of St Procopius ploughing.

The statue of Bruncvík

On the edge of the pier facing outwards is the statue of Bruncvík, the work of the sculptor L. Šimek of 1884.

According to legend Bruncvík was the Czech king who first used the lion in the Czech coat-of-arms. He is believed to have owned a sword of such miraculous properties that by only unsheathing it, he could behead his enemies.

The statue depicts the knight wearing full armour, with a raised sword in his right hand and with the Old Town coat-of-arms at his side. The former statue, now replaced with an inexact copy, stood on the pier at the beginning of the 16th century. It probably represents the statues of so-called "Rolands", which symbolized the market priviliges of the cities.

The statue of St Augustine

The original by J. B. Kohl of 1708 was replaced by this copy by A. Sopr and J. Dušek in 1974. The original statue was financed by the Augustinian Order of St Thomas in the Lesser Quarter.

St Augustine (354—430 AD), the Bishop of Alexandria, was one of the greatest religious philosophers and is the patron saint of the Augustinian Order.

He is depicted with his bishop's mitre and a crosier, in his right hand be he holds a burning heart — a symbol of the Augustinian Order. The child with a conch at his feet symbolizes the infinity of the grace of God. The date on the plinth is 1708.

The statue of St Nicholas of Tolentino

The original by J. B. Kohl of 1708 was replaced by this copy by J. Jiříkovský in 1966. The original statue was paid for by the Augustinian Order of St Thomas.

St Nicholas of Tolentino (†1308), a member of the Augustinian Order, was a renowned preacher and benefactor of the poor. The statue shows him dressed in the Augustinian vesture with a lily, and offering bread from a basket, which is held in front of him by a cherub. The date 1708 is in the cartouche on the plinth.

The statue of St Cajetan

This statue by F. M. Brokoff of 1709 was financed by the Theatine Order.

St Cajetan of Tiene (1480—1547) was co-founder of the Theatine, or Cajetan Order.

In front of the obelisk with cherubs in clouds stands the Saint, dressed in the vesture of the Order, holding a book and a pen. A burning heart is at the top of the obelisk.

The sculpture of St Luitgarde

This work by M. B. Braun of 1710 was financed by E. Tyttl, the Abbot of the Cistercian Monastery at Plasy.

St Luitgarde (†1246) was a nun of the Cistercian Order, who was blind for the last eleven years of her life. Before her death she had a vision, in which Christ on the cross appeared and pressed the wound in his side to her lips.

The figure of St Luitgarde in a state of ecstasy looks up to Christ gliding down towards her from the cross. Cherubs in clouds are to the right of the cross. The sculpture reproduces faithfully the vision of St Luitgarde.

The statue of St Philip Benitius

This statue made from Austrian marble by B. Mandl, a sculptor from Salzburg, originates from 1714 and was paid for by the Order of Servites in Prague.

St Philip Benitius was a member of the Order of Servites, or Servants of the Virgin Mary, and later its fifth General.

The statue depicts the Saint, dressed in the vesture of the Order, with a book, a lily and a crucifix in his left hand.

The statue of St Adalbert

The original by J. M. Brokoff of 1709 was replaced by the copy by V. Hořínek in 1973. The original statue was paid for by M. J. Joanelli, a councillor of the Old Town.

St Adalbert (956—997 AD) of the Slavníkovec dynasty was the second Bishop of Prague. He died as a martyr among the heathen Prussians, where he worked as a missionary. He is considered as a patron of the Czech clergy and is one of Bohemia's patron saints.

He is depicted as a bishop with a mitre and a crosier. The coat-of-arms of the Joanelli family is on the pedestal. The most complicated chronogram on Charles Bridge, in which the year 1709 has to be added together in both parts of the inscription, is on the lower part of the plinth.

The statue of St Vitus

The statue was sculpted by F. M. Brokoff in 1714 and financed by Matěj Vojtěch from

Löwenmacht, the Dean of Vyšehrad.

St Vitus was a Christian martyr, who several times miraculously escaped death (even when he was thrown to the lions) but at the beginning of the 4th century he was tortured to death. Prince Wenceslas obtained some of his relics for St Vitus' Rotunda at Prague Castle, the other relics were brought by Charles IV at the time that St Vitus' Cathedral was built. As he is the Saint, to whom the most important Czech cathedral was consecrated, he is one of Bohemia's patron saints.

The figure dressed as a Roman legionary stands on the pedestal surrounded by lions.

The sculpture of SS. John of Matha, Felix of Valois and Ivan

This work by F. M. Brokoff of 1714 was erected by Count František Josef Thun from Klášterec for the Prague members of the Order of the Most Holy Trinity on the occasion of the 500th anniversary of the death of St John of Matha.

St John of Matha (†1214) founded the Order ot the Most Holy Trinity together with St Felix of Valois. This Order collected money to buy slaves their freedom. The founding of the Order was initiated by a vision, in which St John saw an angel freeing a Christian and a heathen slave from chains. Together with St Felix they then saw a stag with the cross between its antlers.

St Ivan was the next of the Bohemia's patron saints. He lived as a hermit in the forest of Tetín.

The biggest sculpture on Charles Bridge depicts both Trinitarian Saints and their visions — at the front St Felix with a free slave and a cartouche, with the vision of St John on it, St John stands on the rock, and a stag with the cross between its antlers is below him.

St Ivo with a cross above a dead hind,

which was believed to have been caught by the prince Břetislav, forms a complement to the sculpture. The captured Christians, guarded by a Turk with a cat-o'-nine tails, are behind the bars in the pedestal of the sculpture. The date 1714 is on the right of the plinth.

The sculpture of Christ with SS. Cosmas and Damian

The sculpture by J. O. Mayer of 1709 was funded by the Medical Faculty of Prague University.

SS. Cosmas and Damian (†303 AD) were Christian twins, whose medical abilities helped them in successfully converting heathens to Christianity. Their common activities ended in their common martyrdom. They are the patron saints of doctors and pharmacists.

On each side of Christ stand the two martyrs, wearing university gowns and birettas, holding palm branches and medicine vessels. The date 1709 is repeated below each figure of the sculpture and on the cross.

The statue of St Wenceslas

The statue of St Wenceslas by J. K. Böhm was paid for by the Klar Institute of the Blind in 1858.

St Wenceslas, the Přemyslid prince murdered by his brother Boleslav, is the main patron saint of the Bohemian Kingdom.

The statue depicts him in prayer, with a banner, a prince's cap, and a coat-of-arms bearing a spread-eagle.

The relief carving by K. Salzar of 1784 depicts the repair of Charles Bridge after a flood. A plan of Charles Bridge together with the twelve piers of Judith Bridge, which could be seen when the water level was low, form an unusual part of the relief.

516 m long, Charles Bridge spans the Vltava with semi – circular vaulted arches. The humble body of the bridge, giving the impression of firmness and reliability, is laced with Baroque schulptures (left). Standing in the beautiful Knights of the Cross Square with its sculpture of Charles IV of 1848, you enter the bridge through the monumental Old Town Bridge Tower. Sculptural decoration by Peter Parler together with subtle corner turrets help to articulate the block character of the tower and make it one of most beautiful Gothic towers in Europe. The masonry of a white risalit of the Knights of the Cross Hospital standing to the right of Charles Bridge conceals the Old Town Tower of Judith Bridge (right).

Figures of SS. Adalbert *(left)* and Sigismond *(right)* look down from the top floor of the Old Town Bridge Tower, statues of these Czech patron saints resting on picturesque figurative consoles dating back to the 1380s *(left)*.

The main field of decoration on the east front of the Old Town Bridge Tower is dominated by statues of St Vitus *(in the middle),* Charles IV *(on the left), and young* Wenceslas IV *(on the right).* In between the statues of Luxembourg rulers there are two bridge arches with a figure of St Vitus resting on them. On either side of this figure are coats–of–arms with the Imperial spread–eagle *(on the left)* and the Czech Lion *(on the right)* both of them with a complete heraldic set. Below the string – course at first floor level there are emblems of the lands belonging to the Kingdom of Bohemia in the last years of Charles's IV reign. Above St Vitus is a coat–of–arms constaining the spread–eagle of St Wenceslas *(right).*

On top of the staircase in the Old Town Bridge Tower is a sculpture of a so-called "towerman" created in the late 14th century, this naturalistically conceived figure of a hunchback resembling the later, famous bell–ringer of Notre Dame in Paris.

The wooden panelled ceiling of the 2nd floor dates back to the 1850s. Originally it was fitted in the Old Town Hall but in 1880 moved here. Neogothic coats–of–arms of the Czech lands ware painted in the same year.

Sightseers' chiseled inscriptions, pock—marking the staircase of the Old Town Bridge Tower, damage a late Gothic incription written in rust – coloured clay.

Figurative consoles on the Old Town Bridge Tower, depicting animals fighting and surprisingly realistic scenes of every day life in a medieval town, are highly interesting elements of its decoration.

A motif of a kingfisher on a wreath is a typical decorative element of Wenceslas' time. It appears mainly on consructions connected more or less directly with Wenceslas himself. We find it four times on the east front of the tower, while on the west front the motif represents only a small fragment of the original decoration.

The net vault of the archway culminates in a coping – stone resembling a royal crown with a "pouring hole" in its centre. Painted decoration was carried out in 1877 – 1878 by P. Maixner, who faithfully followed the original intentions. As well as heraldic decoration there reappear Wenceslas' kingfisher and a no less popular motif of a female barber – surgeon.

The present appearance of the west front of the Old Town Bridge Tower differs considerably from the original Gothic one. Its significance is represented by a Latin inscription commemorating the repelling of a Swedish attack in 1648. At that time artillery fire completely destroyed its sculptural decoration, which used to be comparable with that of the east front. As a reward for the successful defence of the bridge Ferdinand III enriched the Old Town coat – of – arms with a hand holding a bare sword, this new element being set in an open gate. The new arms form part of the famous Latin inscription, created and set in the tower in 1651 – 1654 by the Italian architect Carlo Lurago.

Standing at the Old Town Bridge Tower we can easily see the slightly S – shaped route of the bridge. The inimitable atmosphere of both the bridge and the panorama of Prague Castle remains, even in winter.

The sculpture of the Madonna and St Bernard *by M. V. Jäckle dating back to 1709. In the middle of the pedestal consisting of angels on clouds stands the Virgin Mary and the Infant Jesus. St Bernard kneels on the left, with an angel in front of him holding his abbot's mitre. On the left there are other angels holding the Crucifix with a versaicon – a shroud bearing a print of Jesus's face. On the pedestal are tools of Christ's crucifixion (left).*

The sculpture of St Ivo *by M. B. Braun of 1711. The figure of the Saint holds the Legal Code in his righ hand and lays his left hand in a protective gesture above a group of his poor clients. On his side stands the allegorical figure of Justice (right).*

The sculpture of the Madonna with SS. Dominic and Thomas Aquinas *by M. V. Jäckl of 1708. The two Dominican Saints, on the left St Dominic and on the right St Thomas, turn towards the Virgin Mary, who stands amid clouds above the globe. The dog with a burning torch in the middle symbolizes the Dominican Order (in Latin-"domini canis" – God's dog), the cherub on his right side holding a bee-hive is a symbol of Thomas' diligence (left).*

The sculpture of SS. Barbara, Margaret and Elizabeth *of 1707 is the work of all three sculptor members of the Brokoff family. The statute of St Barbara with a chalice and a tower by her side is in the middle, St Margaret, the other martyr, and a dragon are on the left. St Elizabeth granting alms is on the right. The statues were probably sculpted by both the younger Brokoffs, the plinth covered completely with ornament was made by their father (right).*

The bronze sculpture of the Holy Cross *of 1657 to 1707 is complemented by the figures of the Virgin Mary (on the left) and the Apostle John (on the right), which were made by E. Max in 1861. The inscriptions in Czech, Latin and German say that the Hebrew inscription around the cross was paid for by an unnamed Prague Jew in 1696 as a punishment for blaspheming against the cross. The golden cartouche at the foot of the cross reminds us of the restoration of the sculpture in 1707 (left).*
The sculpture of the Pietà *by E. Max of 1859. Below the cross the helpless body of Christ is supported by the Virgin Mary, St Mary Margaret kneels on the right. The sorrowful Apostle John stands above the three figures (right).*

The statue of St Anne *by M. V. Jäckl of 1707. St Anne, holding the Infant Jesus on her right arm, looks at the youthful looking Virgin Mary (above left).*
The statute of St Joseph *by J. Max of 1854. Joseph with a lily in his left hand is accompanied by the Infant Jesus, who raises his hand in blessing (above right).*
The sculpture of SS. Cyril and Methodius *by K. Dvořák of 1938. The most recent original statue on Charles Bridge shows the two brothers, Byzantine Missionaries, baptizing three Moravian men (right).*

The sculpture of St Francis Xavier *by F. M. Brokoff of 1711. St Francis, baptizing an Indian ruler, stands at the top of the pedestal supported by the robust figures of a Chinese man, a Tartar, an Indian and a Moor. A young man holding a conch containing water for baptism is on the right, the statue of the other man looking at the scene is supposed to be Brokoff's self-portrait. The sculpture ranks among Brokoff's greatest works (left).*

The statue of St John the Baptist *by J. Max of 1855. The Saint, wearing a sheep's pelt and a coat, holds a golden cross in his left hand. The conch at his side and the cross remind us of the baptism of Christ (above left).*

The statue of St Christopher *by E. Max of 1857. St Christopher with a stick in his left hand carries the Infant Jesus over the river (above right).*

The sculpture of SS. Norbert. Wenceslas and Sigismond *by J. Max of 1853. St
Norbert stands on a neo-Gothic plinth in the centre of a group of three Saints, who are
included among Bohemia's patron saints. Two armed sovereign Saints are at either side
of him – on the left St Wenceslas and on the right St Sigismond.*

The Sculpture of St Francis Borgia *by F. M.*
Brokoff of 1710. The dominant figure of St Francis
is accompanied by a pair of angels holding illustra-
tions of the host and the Virgin Mary.

The statue of St John of Nepomuk *by J. Brokoff of 1683. The bronze sculpture was cast by J. W. Heroldt in Nuremberg after a wooden model by Brokoff. On the plinth is the typical depiction of St John, with the palm branch of a martyr and a crucifix, together with two cast reliefs. Wenceslas IV, in Baroque style, watches his wife Sophia at confession in the first relief, the martyr's death of John of Nepomuk is shown in the second.*

The sculpture of St Ludmila *by M. B. Braun of 1730. St Ludmila with a veil, as a symbol of her martyr's death, teaches little St Wenceslas to read the Bible. The relief depicting the scene of the murder of St Wenceslas is on the plinth (left).*

The statute of St Anthony of Padua *by J. O. Mayer of 1707. The Infant Jesus, standing on a lectern, leans on St Anthony who is holding a lily, and has a halo (right).*

The sculpture of St Francis Seraphicus *by E. Max of 1855. A pair of angels holding the Gospels and a cross, accompany the figure of St Francis, wearing the vestments of the Minorite Order (left).*

The statue of St Jude of Thaddeus *by J. O. Mayer of 1708. One of the Twelve Apostles is depicted here with a book in his right hand, leaning against a large club, the tool of his martyrdom (right).*

The sculpture of SS. Vincent Ferrarius and Procopius *by F. M. Brokoff of 1712. St Vincent (on the left) resuscitates the corpse and St Procopius (on the right) triumphs over the vanquished Satan. The figures of unbelievers and Satan on the plinth bear their conquerors. The reliefs of the Last Judgement and of St Procopius with the devil harnessed to the plauhg are on the plinth (left).*

The statue of Bruncvík *by L. Šimek of 1884. The sculpture, which is an inexact copy of the former work from the beginning of the 16th century, depicts the knight, with a raised sword and the Old Town coat-of-arms at his side, on the plinth with figurative decoration (right).*

51

The statue of St Augustine *by J. B. Kohl of 1708. St Augustine, with a bishop's mitre and a crosier, holds a burning heart — a symbol of the Augustinian Order — in his raised right hand (left).*

The statue of St Nicholas of Tolentino *by J. B. Kohl of 1708. The Saint, dressed in Augustinian vestments with a lily in his left hand, is offering bread from a basket, which is held in front of him by a cherub (right).*

The statue of St Cajetan *by F. M. Brokoff of 1709. A three-sided obelisk with cherubs in clouds and a burning heart at the top is behind the figure of the Saint, dressed in the vestments of the Theatine Order (left).*

The sculpture of St Luitgarde *by M. B. Braun of 1710. The helpless body of Christ is hanging down from the cross towards St Luitgarde, who looks up to him in a state of ecstasy. The sculpture is considered to be the finest work on Charles Bridge (right).*

The statue of St Vitus *by F. M. Brokoff of 1714. St Vitus, dressed as a Roman legionary, stands on a pedestal in the form of a rock, with a number of lions. St Vitus is the patron saint of Bohemia (left).*

The sculpture of SS. John of Matha, Felix of Valois and Ivan *by F. M. Brokoff of 1714. The two founders of the Order of the Most Holy Trinity and their visions are depicted in the upper part of this, the biggest sculpture on Charles Bridge. The hermit St Ivan, the other patron saint of Bohemia complements the two other figures. Captured Christian slaves, for whom this Order helped to buy liberty, are behind bars inside a cavity in the pedestal. The Christian slaves are guarded by the Turk with a cat-o'-nine tails (right).*

The sculpture of Christ with SS. Cosmas and Damian *by J. O. Mayer of 1709. On both sides of Christ are two very similar figures — two martyred brothers — with medicine vessels, a symbol of their medical activities (left).*

The statue of St Wenceslas *by J. K. Böhm of 1858. The Přemyslid prince, the first of Bohemia's patron saints, is depicted as a warrior in prayer (right).*

One of the classic views of the Lesser Quarter end of Charles Bridge shows not only the sculpture of St Luitgarde by M. Braun and both Lesser Quarter Bridge Towers but also other dominant features of the left bank of the Vltava — the Church of St Nicholas and Prague Castle (left).
Charles Bridge leads into the Lesser Quarter between a pair of bridge towers. On a battlement above the gate we notice from the left — the Luxembourg Lioness, the Czech Lion with two tails and the Moravian spread-eagle. The Old Town coat-of-arms below the gargoyle was placed on the tower later (right).

The archivolt of the eastern facade of the gate between the Lesser Quarter towers is supported by brackets, decorated with fabulous animals.

The relief on the eastern side of the smaller Lesser Quarter Bridge Tower is a masterpiece of Czech Romanesque sculpture. Partial erosion of both figures makes it impossible for us to determine explicitly who the enthroned and kneeling figures depict. It is probable that a Romanesque artist of around 1170 depicted the granting of the royal title to the Bohemian Prince Vladislav II by Emperor Fridrich Barbarossa, which took place at Regensburg in 1158.

A series of reliefs on the ashlar blocks of the smaller Lesser Quarter Bridge Tower were probably carved during the stay of the soldiers of the later King Přemysl Otakar II, who entrenched himself here in 1249 against his father Wenceslas I. Among simple reliefs of human faces, symbols and animals, a finely carved relief with a running dog stands out.

The Old Town Bridge Tower stood as an example for the higher Lesser Quarter Bridge Tower. A chisel-shaped roof, bartizans connected by battlements and a tripartite architectural frame for the sculptural decoration, which was not added, follow the example of Parler's tower.

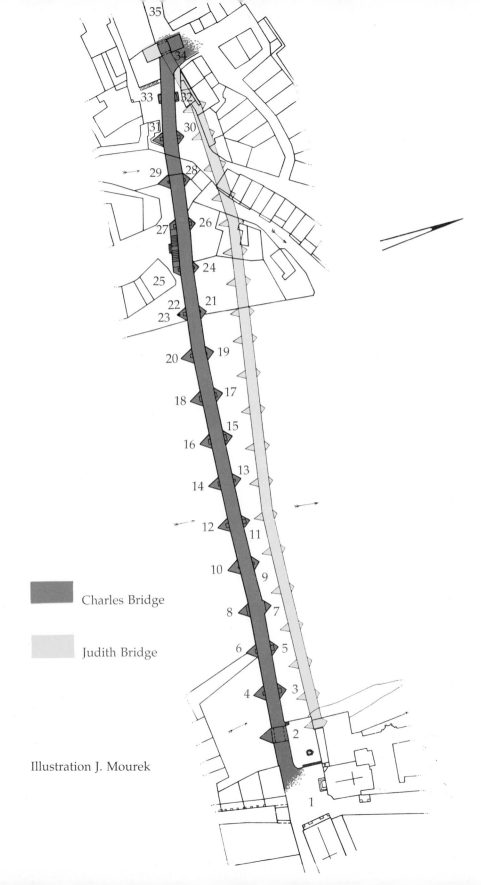

Charles Bridge

Judith Bridge

Illustration J. Mourek

Chronological summary